THIS BC

To personalize your handbook, attach your pet's photo here so it shows through the cover.

THE CAT-SITTER'S HANDBOOK

A Personalized Guide for Your Pet's Caregiver

KAREN ANDERSON

Willow Creek
P R E S S

© 2001 Karen Anderson

Published by Willow Creek Press, P.O. Box 147, Minocqua, Wisconsin 54548

Design by Patricia Bickner Linder

For information on other Willow Creek Press titles, call 1-800-850-9453

Library of Congress Cataloging-in-Publication Data
Anderson, Karen
The cat sitter's handbook : a personalized guide for your pet's caregiver /
by Karen Anderson.
p. cm.
ISBN 1-57223-401-6 (hardcover)
1. Cats—Handbooks, manuals, etc. 2. Pet sitting—Handbooks,
manuals, etc. 3. Diaries. I. Title
SF442 .A535 2001
636.8--dc21
2001000112

Printed in U.S.A.

CONTENTS

PART ONE

JUST FOR
THE
CAT OWNER

WHY YOUR CAT NEEDS A CAT-SITTER WHEN YOU GO AWAY

If you could ask your cat where he'd like to stay (and with whom) when you're gone on vacation, and if your cat could answer you, he'd probably say something like, "Actually, I'd like to convince you to just forget the trip and stay home with me!" In other words, your kitty won't get real excited about spending the time you're away with anyone. He prefers you and he will miss you terribly. With that in mind, it's a good idea to make kitty's time away from you as pleasant as possible; kitty will be in a better mood when you return and you will enjoy the satisfying feeling that you did everything possible to make life easier for your feline friend!

HOME-SWEET-HOME

Although fine cat kennels and "kitty condo" boarding houses do exist, nothing can replace home as the best and least-traumatic place to leave your cat when you go away. Uprooting kitty from his beloved territory and familiar surroundings is usually quite upsetting and could instill in him unnecessary fears and distrust. Depression or anxiety can easily set in and a cat may refuse to eat. Kitty may endure his stay at the local cat motel seemingly well and come through the ordeal with little noticeable resentment, but you can be sure that he or she did not enjoy the experience by any stretch of the imagination.

THE CASE FOR AND AGAINST DROP-IN CAT-SITTERS

Once you've decided to let your cat stay in her warm and cozy home, you may be wondering if you can simply leave kitty there alone and have a neighbor look in on her once in a while to replenish her food and water bowls. The answer is "no" ... but also "yes," providing you really, really must. Certainly a cat who is left alone in her own familiar house (without a live-in cat-sitter) is better off than a cat who is hauled off to a foreign place with lots of strange cats, unfamiliar people, and new scents, but you'd be giving your cat second best by not offering the kind of meaningful, daily interaction a human house-mate would provide.

It's possible too, that a person who merely checks on your cat now and then will forget to visit regularly or let other things

8

get in the way of coming to see kitty. Live-in cat-sitters return to your home each day to eat and sleep and thus, will consistently and predictably spend time with the cat. It is certainly not cruel to utilize the services of a "drop-in" cat-sitter if you truly cannot locate a live-in cat-sitter, but be aware that you may be jeopardizing kitty's state of mind and heart. It's worth it to find your cat a faithful, feline-loving friend!

WHAT MAKES A
GOOD CAT-SITTER?

So, how do you sleuth out a great live-in cat-sitter? There's a good chance that you already know several people who might be excellent candidates for your cat-sitter. It helps to find a decided "cat lover" but this is not a prerequisite. Often cat-sitting will introduce someone to the wonderful world of the feline and a new cat lover is born! The cat-sitter must definitely like cats and be completely open to exploring the ways of the feline, but he or she needn't be an expert or necessarily have lots of experience with cats.

Obviously, if you are successful at locating a self-proclaimed cat lover, don't hesitate to enlist him or her — what a gift you will be giving to your cat! What one usually finds however, is that most cat lovers are unable to come to your home and cat-sit

10

because they are busy staying at home with their own cats! At any rate, begin looking about, asking around and consulting your address book for suitable prospects; and always allow plenty of time before you plan to leave on vacation to line up your cat's companion.

CAT-CONSCIENTIOUS

When choosing a cat-sitter, the single most important quality you need to look for is a strong sense of responsibility. The person who stays with your cat is going to be the person who makes sure kitty is safe, healthy and happy while you're away. For instance, you will want to avoid the type who is likely to leave the back door open and let the cat escape; or someone who forgets to keep certain windows closed that kitty may jump from. Your cat-sitter needs to take his or her job pretty seriously, and you need to be assured he does. Hey, the welfare of your precious feline is what's at stake here!

A HOME-BODY TYPE

Part of the reason you are obtaining a cat-sitter is to provide your beloved cat with someone to connect with while you're gone. If the cat-sitter is constantly on the go and rarely home or away for long stretches at a time (more than the regular workday), kitty will suffer from loneliness and won't be too thrilled. You can't ask an individual to remain home every day and night, but you can inquire how often they spend their free time just hanging out at home. It's perfectly all right to share your expectations for (roughly) how much time kitty will have the cat-sitter's company.

REFERRED AND PREFERRED

Often, the very best way to find a cat-sitter is through a friend or acquaintance. Inquire of neighbors, friends, co-workers, fellow church and club members, relatives and even your cat's vet. Single or "unattached" folks are most frequently used (for reasons clear) and young adults who live at home with the folks are great choices, as they are usually happy to stay on their own for a while. Call around and persistently stick with the search! Once you've obtained a couple of good leads, set up interviews with your prospective cat-sitters and ask direct questions to discern their habits. Get to know them and allow them to get to know you; their cat-sitting stint will seem more like staying at a new friend's house — and this is beneficial for everyone!

PART TWO

CAT AT A GLANCE

IMPORTANT INFORMATION
ABOUT OUR CAT(S)

Veterinarian _____

address _____

_____

phone # _____

The cat carrier is kept (just in case) _____

The food is kept _____

The litter box is in the _____

Cat's name/breed _____

age/date of birth _____   M   F   neutered?_____

feed _____ scoop(s) per day at ____ AM ____PM

medication(s)* _____

administer at _____

*Please also read the information on pages 19 and 43.

Cat's name/breed _____

age/date of birth _____ **M F** neutered?_____

feed _____ scoop(s) per day at ____ AM ____ PM

medication(s)* _____

administer at _____

Cat's name/breed _____

age/date of birth _____ **M F** neutered?_____

feed _____ scoop(s) per day at ____ AM ____ PM

medication(s)* _____

administer at _____

Cat's name/breed _____

age/date of birth _____ **M F** neutered?_____

feed _____ scoop(s) per day at ____ AM ____ PM

medication(s)* _____

administer at _____

17

EVERYTHING YOU EVER WANTED TO KNOW ABOUT OUR CAT(S) BUT DIDN'T NEED TO ASK BECAUSE WE WROTE IT DOWN

Where does kitty sleep? _____

_____

What is kitty's personality like? _____

_____

_____

_____

_____

_____

Does your cat have an illness I should know about? _____

_____

_____

If you've left medications for kitty, how do I best administer?* _____

_____

_____

_____

_____

Does kitty have nicknames or endearing names it loves to hear? _____

_____

What are some favorite games? _____

_____

_____

_____

Can kitty have a food treat now and then? Of what? How often? _____

_____

_____

Does your cat like to be picked up? _____

_____

*Please also read the information on page 43.

How can I get kitty to warm up to me? _____

_____

_____

Does your cat enjoy brushing? A massage or neck rub? _____

_____

_____

Should I treat the house with any flea products while you're gone? _____

_____

What do I do if kitty spits up a hairball? _____

_____

What is off-limits to kitty in this house? How do I (try to) enforce it?

_____

_____

_____

_____

_____

Can I ever let your cat outside? _____

_____

What are the outside boundaries (backyard, on leash, etc.)? _____

_____

_____

Do I need to clean out the litter box? _____

_____

Supplies are kept where? _____

_____

What interior doors should be kept open?_____

_____

Are there certain windows that should remain closed? _____

_____

If I cannot find the cat (inside or out), what do you recommend I do?

_____

_____

How do the multiple cats in this household interact? Are they likely to fight? Play-fight? Hiss? Growl? Curl up together? _____

_____

_____

_____

_____

_____

What do I need to know about the territory balance between cats? _____

_____

_____

_____

_____

_____

_____

Does kitty have any behavioral peculiarities I should know about? _____

_____

_____

_____

_____

_____

Please mention anything else I should know about your cat(s): _____

_____

_____

_____

_____

_____

_____

_____

HOW TO REACH THE CAT OWNERS
AND WHEN THEY'LL BE BACK

Date/time you'll be returning?	Do you wish me to be here upon your arrival home?	What phone numbers can you be reached at on this trip?

PART THREE

JUST FOR THE CAT-SITTER

AN ESSENTIAL ORIENTATION TO CATS

Okay. So you are the chosen cat-sitter for the cat (or cats) in this household while the people who live here are away. You might be staying for a few days, a couple of weeks, or even a month or longer. Perhaps you have lots of experience with cats and relate to them quite well — even magnificently. However, it could be that you find yourself fairly green when it comes to the feline persuasion and you wouldn't mind an easily digestible tip or two. Whichever level of cat savvy you claim, the next few pages will help you immensely during your stay. Worry not, this won't be painful or difficult — it may actually be fun!

The idea is to understand what generally makes the cat tick so that you and the furry feline in your care aren't clawing the

walls with frustration or going mad with boredom, simply endur-
ing the days and hours until the cat owner returns. Regardless of
your prior cat encounters, it is very possible that this time, things
will go more smoothly and enjoyably than ever. And hey, you
just may become a "cat-person" . . . if you aren't one already.

THE UNIQUE PSYCHE OF A CAT

The cat, while proudly holding the title of most common pet
in the U.S., is extraordinarily unique and vastly misunder-
stood. Whatever you do, don't treat the cat like a dog. Alright,
so you don't plan to treat the cat like a dog and you are 99 percent
sure that you wouldn't treat the cat like a dog, but unfortunately,
the tendency is quite common — especially for dog lovers.

It happens innocently enough, as subconscious dog-thoughts
creep into the mind and you hear yourself muttering things like,

"Why is this cat so uncooperative?" or "Why is kitty so aloof — I don't think she even likes me!" You might even notice yourself comparing cats to dogs and concluding that cats seem to come up short. If this sounds familiar, you're not alone. Dog-lovers relatively new to the world of cats often struggle with understanding cat behavior.

WHO'S THE BOSS?

The first thing to remember is that cats lack the "cooperation" gene that dogs have hard-wired into them. The concept of "obedience" is completely meaningless to the feline — it's just not there! While dogs trot through life with a bent towards obeying the master, cats stride along as astonishingly autonomous creatures. A cat won't do a single thing that it does not wish to do! This takes a bit of getting used to, especially if you're accustomed to dogs. Wild dogs move in packs and highly value team spirit. Without this strong instinct to coordinate with others and respond to commands, wild and domestic cats operate in blissful independence, even though they may spend time with other cats or people. In other words, you cannot expect the cat to follow your orders — comforting, isn't it? The best you can do is win its respect and make suggestions.

GREAT CAPACITY FOR FRIENDSHIP

Cats will form meaningful connections with each other out of desire for companionship, comfort, or affection, but never out of a sense of duty or obligation. Kitty views you in much the same way. With a cat, there's a trust that must form before kitty decides to invest in friendship. Unlike dogs, cats don't usually approach a person with the innocent-until-proven-guilty stance.

29

Often it takes a bit of time to cultivate a really special relationship with a feline, but once you're in . . . you're in and you'll know it! Remember, the cat won't be falling all over you like a dog; instead, you will be treated to more subtle expressions of affection. Look out for a rub of the cheek, the soft tail weaving around your legs, the cat sitting near you or on you, and maybe some contented purrs and sweet murmurings.

It helps to know that some cats can be coy and cautious about showing affection towards people. What appears to be ambivalence may actually be shyness or insecurity, not aloofness or feelings of superiority — as is often touted! Resist any temptation to give up on kitty and assume she's not interested in spending time with you. Try asking the cat to follow you around, jump onto your lap, on the bed, etc., and keep asking, to let her know that you'd really like her company. Pat the place on your lap, scratch the spot on the sofa, make up little ways to call her; you'll be amazed!

The key to friendship with a feline is R-E-S-P-E-C-T. Cats can sense what you think about them and they've got to be absolutely sure that you respect their felineness. Cats are sensitive, emotional animals who need reassurance and lots of praise and affirmation. Even in the short time you will be staying with the cat in this house, a delightful friendship can blossom.

HOW TO PLAY WITH KITTY

There's really just one priceless tip that should govern all the playing you do with the cat: hunting practice! That's right — all you need to do is ascertain which games will stimulate a particular cat's instinct to hunt. Keep in mind that cats always get to play the part of the chaser . . . never, never the one being chased. (Failure to follow this rule

may seriously undermine your budding relationship with the cat
— and may risk damage to a delicate feline psyche.)

A SLOWER APPROACH

Don't expect the cat to play as long as a dog would, for
instance, because it's just not going to happen. Cats are not
lazy as some would assert, but they do pace themselves through
life and are careful not to overexert. (The reason is because they
want to be ready at any second to plunge into a chase or an
attack. This is also why cats require so much sleep — at least 12
hours each day.) Most cats are up for a rousing play session 3
or 5 times each day — especially if enthusiastic humans get
involved and initiate the games. Watch for what kitty does when
she seems to be wishing to play . . . if she's batting the viney
plant tendrils, then find a piece of something to pull around and

flip up. If she's knocking pens off the counter or other items off the edges of a surface, then find something unbreakable and create a similar game. You get the picture. Hopefully, notes left by the cat owner will be helpful in the "feline fun" department. Consult the list below for a few ideas and the golden rules of kitty playtime.

PURRFECT PLAY

* Pull a ribbon, soft belt or flexible tape measure along the floor — starting and stopping it like a real critter would move! Tie interesting things on the end (like netting or piece of mylar ribbon), but be sure not to let kitty get it loose and swallow it.

* Make one-inch foil balls to throw and let kitty chase — some cats will retrieve them!

✳ Sneak little fake mice around. Get them to peek out from under a sheet, rug or cushion. Watch out for eager claws!

✳ Scoot pens and pencils around and under the edges of papers and desk edges when you're at the computer — it's a great way to keep the paws off "delete" and "exit."

✳ Find a large paper bag or cardboard box and place it on the floor for the cat to investigate. Tap the outside of the bag or box once the cat is inside.

✳ Get out the catnip toy and play keep-away for a while before letting kitty have it.

THE 3 NO-NO'S

1 Never chase the cat — this instills unnecessary fears and possible aggression.

2 Don't pretend to attack the cat — it will think that you are truly out to get it.

3 Don't tease the cat — it won't understand or appreciate it.

ENFORCING THE RULES

Be sure and refer to the Everything-You-Ever-Wanted-to-Know-About-Our-Cat pages at the front of this handbook to get familiar with the owner's house rules and most effective ways of disciplining this particular cat. Don't overdo the discipline — always err on the side of less. Cats are very sensitive and a little reminding goes a long way.

Most cat owners will list only a few places or things that are taboo for the cat, such as getting on kitchen counters and tables, or scratching furniture and rugs. The only other problem that may require discipline is any kind of aggression or lashing out towards you or your guests. Most likely, this isn't going to happen. Any cat owner who has purchased this book and made the effort to obtain your services has probably nurtured the cat well, and given him no reason to seriously act out.

TOUGH AND TENDER

The feline spirit is indomitable on the one hand, yet quite fragile on the other. Cats possess an impressive inner confidence which carries them through an awful lot in life, but don't let that resilient front fool you! Beneath the self-assurance and strong, capable instincts lies an extremely vulnerable creature whose feelings are easily bruised. This means that when the cat's behavior warrants a touch of discipline, the trick is to somehow convince kitty that, while what he did was very bad, he is still very good. The psychology here is not unlike that which parents use on their children. It's a delicate balancing act and bit of work, but worth it!

THINK GENTLE

Any harsh movement, prolonged yelling or growling at the cat can be damaging. Instead of gaining the cat's respectful attention you will only cause him to fear you — ending up with a frightened or a vicious cat. Remember, a cat who feels attacked in any way is going to react negatively and unpredictably (even if you didn't intend to appear aggressive). Plus, he will certainly not learn from it. Stay calm, act swiftly, and surround any disciplinary moment with lots of loving and forgiving affirmation.

THE DO'S AND DON'TS OF DISCIPLINE

Here is the cardinal rule not to be broken at any cost: NEVER hit the cat. There is no circumstance where striking a cat is justified — none. Instead there are 3 safe, proven methods of on-the-spot discipline that are highly effective and do not injure the psyche of the feline. First, try to convince kitty to stop what it's doing with a gentle "no-no." That may suffice.

Resort to the methods below only if your words don't work. In all three options, cats hate the sensation, but it does no harm.

1 THE SPRAY BOTTLE. (The cat Owner should have left one for you but if not, go splurge a buck or two.) Waiting not longer than 10 seconds after the cat does the bad thing, softly spray some water right at kitty 1-3 times.

2 THE POUF. Waiting not longer than 10 seconds after the cat does the bad thing, take a deep breath and blow one or two short, forceful poufs right into kitty's face.

3 THE SHOUT. Waiting not longer than 10 seconds after the cat does the bad thing, let out one very loud, very shrill word such as: NO! or STOP! or HEY! Try very hard not to use kitty's name and don't keep yelling after the initial shout.

GENERAL RULES FOR DISCIPLINE

✳ Do be consistent.

✳ Do reserve reminders for the things that really count in the household.

✳ Do praise kitty profusely for responding to reminders and requests.

✳ Do give out food treats (if okay with owner) for positive behavior.

✳ Do remember that the cat is an incredibly intelligent and surprisingly sensitive animal!

MEDICATIONS AND EMERGENCIES

IN CASE OF AN EMERGENCY

Of course in any true emergency with the cat, you should phone the vet immediately. If it's after hours, don't worry — you'll reach either an answering service who will contact the doctor or an emergency phone number to handle late-night or weekend problems. Once you have a veterinarian on the phone, describe the cat's symptoms accurately. Follow the doctor's advice and carry out medical instructions carefully. If the vet asks you to bring the cat in, be sure to use the cat carrier for the trip; the last thing you want is a sick, escaped kitty. If you are unable to locate a cat carrier, a sturdy cardboard or plastic box with a lid and airholes will do. The idea is to find something secure in which to keep the cat safe. If the vet is not alarmed and suggests watching kitty at home for a while, then nurse the cat as best you can. Refer to any cat books you might find on the bookshelf and keep in touch with the doctor. You may or may not wish to immediately let the cat owner know of kitty's condition, but certainly get in touch with them if they have left instructions to do so or if the cat's life or well-being appears to be in danger.

GIVING THE CAT MEDS

While it's unlikely you'll encounter an actual emergency while cat-sitting, you may need to give the cat his or her medications for an illness or some other condition. Don't be intimidated by this — all it requires are a few tips and a heaping dose of confidence. If the kitty in your care needs to be "pilled" during your stay, then you've probably had this procedure demonstrated to you by the owner, but if not, here's what to do.

PILLS: Plan to work quickly, gently, and confidently. Pretend you're an expert, and kitty will sense that you know what you're doing and that you are to be trusted. Don't use jerky motions. Act deliberately and quickly; the element of surprise is crucial and may determine your success. Depending upon the cat, you'll want to either take it in your lap or approach it while it's sitting or lying down. With one hand, cradle the cat's head and tilt it far back. With either the same hand or your other hand, place two fingers at the corners of kitty's mouth and pry the mouth open; this won't be difficult, as it will be an involuntary reflex. Just a split second after you have the cat's mouth open, with head still tilted back in your other hand, use the free hand to plop the pill onto the tongue at the very back of the mouth. Then immediately close the jaw firmly and keep the head tilted back, stroking kitty's throat to encourage swallowing.

If you let the cat open its mouth prematurely, it could spit out the pill and you'll be back to square one. To ease swallowing the pill, try coating it with butter or margarine. Remember to be quick, smooth, and positive. You'll be pilling like the professionals in no time.

LIQUIDS: Administering liquid meds from a syringe or tube works similarly to pills, except that a couple more seconds are needed to empty the syringe into kitty's mouth. Cats do not usually resist swallowing the liquid and may even like the taste!

WATCHING FOR SIGNS OF DISTRESS

Most likely you have begun your cat-sitting stint with a healthy cat (or cats) and this fabulous feline is going to stay that way. There are medical problems that could arise however, and you should know what to watch for. As always, never hesitate to phone the vet's office if you're concerned or simply curious about a particular symptom or behavior.

The most important thing to observe is the cat's eating and drinking habits. A healthy cat should be eating all or most of its food and visiting the water bowl a few times each day. You should be concerned if kitty stops eating or drinking for more than two days — a cat must not go without water for longer than three days or the kidneys may suffer serious, life-threatening damage. If this does occur, call the vet or, better yet, take the cat in. If the cat you're watching is missing its owner terribly, it may choose to protest by eating very little or nothing at all for a day or so. It may also drink a bit less water. This is normal for some cats and can usually be turned around with a bit of time and the loving presence of someone like you to soothe the heartsick feline.

Other signs of possible distress are limping, lethargy, vomiting, diarrhea, extreme thirst and blood in the urine. Call the vet if these or any other questionable symptoms persist more than one or two days.

PART FOUR

THE CAT-SITTER'S FEEDBACK PAGES

THE CAT-SITTER'S TURN

Date/Occasion of Owner's Absence _____

_____

Cat-Sitter's Name _____

The cat finished his food __ never __ hardly __ some __ always

Kitty jumped onto my lap __ lots __ some __ rarely __ never

The cat spent most of the time _____

_____

_____

_____

_____

_____

Kitty usually slept on/in the _____

_____

I brushed kitty _____ times.

Most of the time the cat seemed _____ (content, quiet, lonely, sad, happy, confused, bored, scared, other).

Kitty surprised me by _____

_____

_____

_____

The cat meowed __ a lot __ a little __ hardly ever __ never

She mostly meowed when _____

_____

_____

_____

We got along _____ (famously, great, okay, so-so, not great, poorly). Explain _____

_____

_____

_____

A frustrating thing about cat-sitting your cat was _____

_____

_____

_____

_____

The best things about staying with your kitty were _____

_____

_____

_____

_____

I disciplined kitty for _____

_____

_____

_____

I discovered this about your cat _____

_____

_____

_____

You forgot to tell me _____

_____

_____

_____

I'd like to cat-sit for you __ soon __ next yr __ maybe __ not again.

Here's why _____

_____

_____

If I'm unable to cat-sit the next time, here's the name and phone number

for someone I know who may be interested in staying with your cat.

_____

_____

THE CAT-SITTER'S TURN

Date/Occasion of Owner's Absence _____

_____

Cat-Sitter's Name _____

The cat finished his food __ never __ hardly __ some __ always.

Kitty jumped onto my lap __ lots __ some __ rarely __ never.

The cat spent most of the time _____

_____

_____

_____

_____

_____

Kitty usually slept on/in the _____

_____

I brushed kitty _____ times.

Most of the time the cat seemed _____ (content, quiet, lonely, sad, happy, confused, bored, scared, other).

Kitty surprised me by _____

_____

_____

_____

The cat meowed __ a lot __ a little __ hardly ever __ never

She mostly meowed when _____

_____

_____

_____

We got along _____ (famously, great, okay, so-so, not great, poorly). Explain _____

_____

_____

_____

_____

A frustrating thing about cat-sitting your cat was _____

_____

_____

_____

_____

_____

The best things about staying with your kitty were _____

_____

_____

_____

_____

_____

I disciplined kitty for _____

_____

_____

_____

I discovered this about your cat _____

_____

_____

_____

You forgot to tell me _____

_____

_____

_____

I'd like to cat-sit for you __ soon __ next yr __ maybe __ not again.
Here's why _____

_____

_____

If I'm unable to cat-sit the next time, here's the name and phone number
for someone I know who may be interested in staying with your cat.

_____

_____

THE CAT-SITTER'S TURN

Date/Occasion of Owner's Absence _____

_____

Cat-Sitter's Name _____

The cat finished his food __ never __ hardly __ some __ always.

Kitty jumped onto my lap __ lots __ some __ rarely __ never.

The cat spent most of the time _____

_____

_____

_____

_____

Kitty usually slept on/in the _____

_____

I brushed kitty _____ times.

Most of the time the cat seemed _____ (content, quiet, lonely, sad, happy, confused, bored, scared, other).

Kitty surprised me by _____

_____

_____

The cat meowed __ a lot __ a little __ hardly ever __ never

She mostly meowed when _____

_____

_____

_____

We got along _____ (famously, great, okay, so-so, not great, poorly). Explain _____

_____

_____

_____

A frustrating thing about cat-sitting your cat was _____

_____

_____

_____

_____

The best things about staying with your kitty were _____

_____

_____

_____

_____

I disciplined kitty for _____

_____

_____

_____

I discovered this about your cat _____

_____

_____

_____

You forgot to tell me _____

_____

_____

_____

I'd like to cat-sit for you __ soon __ next yr __ maybe __ not again.

Here's why _____

_____

_____

If I'm unable to cat-sit the next time, here's the name and phone number
for someone I know who may be interested in staying with your cat.

_____

_____

THE CAT-SITTER'S TURN

Date/Occasion of Owner's Absence _____

_____

Cat-Sitter's Name _____

The cat finished his food __ never __ hardly __ some __ always.

Kitty jumped onto my lap __ lots __ some __ rarely __ never.

The cat spent most of the time _____

_____

_____

_____

_____

_____

Kitty usually slept on/in the _____

_____

I brushed kitty _____ times.

Most of the time the cat seemed _____ (content, quiet, lonely,
sad, happy, confused, bored, scared, other).

Kitty surprised me by _____

_____

_____

_____

The cat meowed __ a lot __ a little __ hardly ever __ never

She mostly meowed when _____

_____

_____

_____

We got along _____ (famously, great, okay, so-so, not great,
poorly). Explain _____

_____

_____

_____

A frustrating thing about cat-sitting your cat was _____

_____

_____

_____

_____

The best things about staying with your kitty were _____

_____

_____

_____

_____

I disciplined kitty for _____

_____

_____

_____

I discovered this about your cat _____

_____

_____

_____

You forgot to tell me _____

_____

_____

_____

I'd like to cat-sit for you __ soon __ next yr __ maybe __ not again.

Here's why _____

_____

_____

If I'm unable to cat-sit the next time, here's the name and phone number

for someone I know who may be interested in staying with your cat.

_____

_____

EMERGENCY INFORMATION

Veterinarian_____

address _____

_____

phone # _____

Please refer to page 24 for our current whereabouts!

Other (local) emergency contact _____

_____

_____

ABOUT YOUR HOUSE

Where is the main water shut-off valve? _____

Where is the electrical breaker/fuse box? _____

Do you have a spare set of house keys? Where are they kept? ____

_____

64